Table of Co

D1193705

The Bakery 4

You Try It! 24

Solve the Problem 28

Glossary 30

Answer Key 32

This is a bakery.

The Bakery

Subtraction

Lisa Greathouse

Consultants

Chandra C. Prough, M.S.Ed.
National Board Certified
Newport-Mesa
  Unified School District

Jodene Smith, M.A.
ABC Unified School District

Publishing Credits

Dona Herweck Rice, *Editor-in-Chief*
Lee Aucoin, *Creative Director*
Chris McIntyre, M.A.Ed., *Editorial Director*
James Anderson, M.S.Ed., *Editor*
Aubrie Nielsen, M.S.Ed., *Associate Education Editor*
Neri Garcia, *Senior Designer*
Stephanie Reid, *Photo Editor*
Rachelle Cracchiolo, M.S.Ed., *Publisher*

Image Credits

p.3 KRT/Newscom; p.4–5 fotofrog/iStockphoto; p.6 Charles Islander/iStockphoto; p.16 BigStockPhoto; p.24 Getty Images; p.26 Rich Legg/iStockphoto; p.27 iStockphoto; All other images: Shutterstock

Teacher Created Materials

5301 Oceanus Drive
Huntington Beach, CA 92649-1030
http://www.tcmpub.com
ISBN 978-1-4333-3435-1
© 2012 Teacher Created Materials, Inc.
BP 5028

3 treats

1 is sold.
Subtract!

$$3 - 1 = 2$$

2 are **left**.

0 1 2 3 4 5 6 7 8 9 10

4 cakes

2 are sold.
Subtract!

$$4 - 2 = 2$$

2 are left.

0 1 2 3 4 5 6 7 8 9 10

2 cupcakes

1 is sold.
Subtract!

$$2 - 1 = 1$$

1 is left.

0 — 1 — 2 — 3 — 4 — 5 — 6 — 7 — 8 — 9 — 10

5 donuts

4 are sold.
Subtract!

$$5 - 4 = 1$$

1 is left.

0 1 2 3 4 5 6 7 8 9 10

8 pies

4 are sold.
Subtract!

$$8 - 4 = 4$$

4 are left.

6 muffins

6 are sold.

Subtract!

$$6 - 6 = 0$$

0 are left.

10 bagels

6 are sold.
Subtract!

10 − 6 = 4

4 are left.

7 cookies

3 are sold.
Subtract!

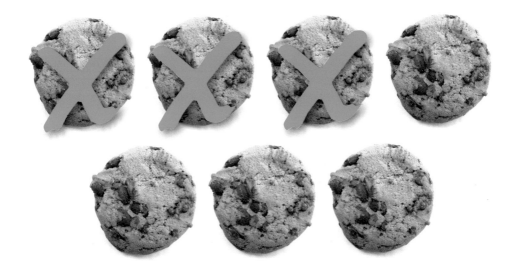

$$7 - 3 = 4$$

4 are left.

6 slices of bread

1 is sold.
Subtract!

$$6 - 1 = 5$$

5 are left.

There are 4 cookies.

The boy eats 1.

Subtract!

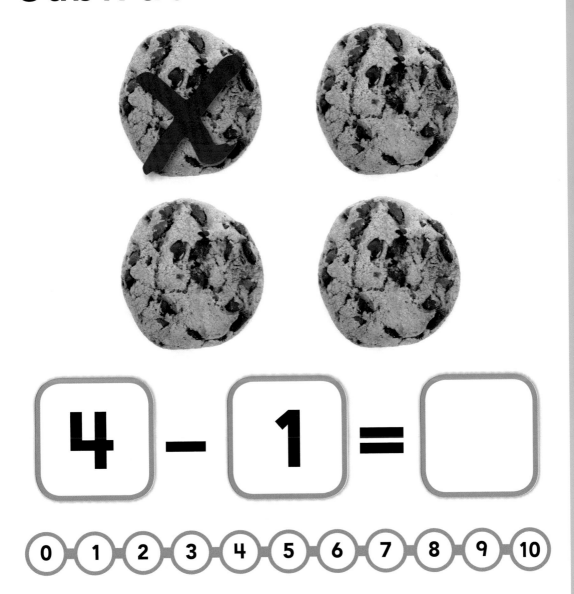

There are 7 slices of cake.

The kids eat 5.

Subtract!

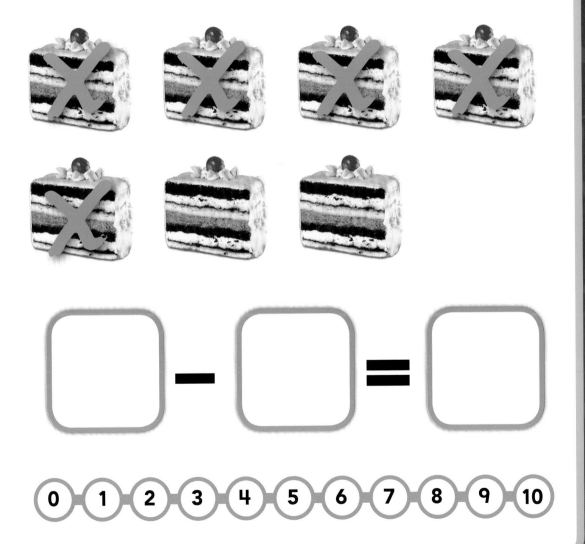

The kids have 8 crackers. They eat 6 crackers. How many crackers are left?

Materials

✓ paper

✓ pencil

1 Draw 8 crackers.

2 Cross out the number of crackers the kids ate.

3 Subtract. Write a number sentence to show your answer.

Glossary

left—still there

$$4 - 2 = \boxed{2}$$

subtract—to take away part of an amount

2 – 1 = 1

You Try It!

Pages 24–25:
4 – 1 = 3
Three (3) cookies are left.

0 1 2 3 4 5 6 7 8 9 10

Pages 26–27:
7 – 5 = 2
Two (2) pieces of cake are left.

0 1 2 3 4 5 6 7 8 9 10

Solve the Problem

Drawings may vary but should show 8 crackers with 6 crossed out. 8 – 6 = 2